D1080241

SLIP STREAM

SUPER ANIMALS

ANNE ROONEY

LONDON•SYDNEY

First published in 2012 by
Franklin Watts
338 Euston Road
London NW1 3BH

Franklin Watts Australia
Level 17/207 Kent Street
Sydney NSW 2000

ISBN 978 1 4451 1308 1

Dewey Classification number: 428.6

A CIP catalogue record for this book is available from the British Library.

Series Editors: Adrian Cole and Jackie Hamley
Series Advisors: Diana Bentley and Dee Reid
Series Designer: Peter Scoulding

Printed in China

Franklin Watts is a division of Hachette Children's Books, an Hachette UK company.
www.hachette.co.uk

Acknowledgements:
AAA Collection/Alamy: 18b.
Barcroft Media/Getty Images: 5.
Miles Barton /Nature PL: 8c, 9b.
Bill 2499/Dreamstime: 23.
Ryan M Boulton/Shutterstock: 14b.
Tony Brindley/Dreamstime: 16c.
Jeff Crabert /Shutterstock: front cover.
Brooks Elliott/istockphoto: 17.
Michael & Patricia Fogden/FLPA: 14.
Jurgen Freund/Nature PL: 4c.
Gail Johnson /Shutterstock: 16t.
Micha Klootwijk/Shutterstock: 22b.
lightpoet/Shutterstock: 21b.
Nature Production /Nature PL: 9t.
Ho New/Reuters: 10b, 11.
Ninamalyna/Dreamstime: 19.
Ben Piek/Dreamstime: 7.
Premphoto/Nature PL: 12c, 13.
Shattil & Rozinski/Nature PL: 1, 20.
supertrooper/Shutterstock: 4b, 8b, 12b, 16b.
Vilaincrevette/Shutterstock: 6b.
worldwildlifewonders/Shutterstock: 21t.

Every attempt has been made to clear copyright. Should there be any inadvertent omission, please apply to the publisher for rectification.

CONTENTS

SUPER ANIMALS

Some animals have super clever tricks!

This octopus hides in a coconut shell. It is safe here!

The angler fish lives in the deep sea. It is dark there. So the fish makes its own light.

SEA CUCUMBER

The sea cucumber has a clever trick. It can make its body turn runny.

Then it can slip into gaps and hide from danger.

CLEVER CROW

This crow likes to eat hard nuts.
But it cannot open them. So the
clever crow drops the nuts on a road.

Cars crush the nuts.
Then the crow can eat them.

FROG CLAWS

When it is in danger, the hairy African frog breaks the bones in its toes.

The bones cut through the skin. They make sharp claws.

GREEDY SPIDERS

Baby black lace-weaver spiders are greedy. They eat the eggs of their brothers and sisters.

Then they eat their mother!

DEAD SNAKE

When the hognose snake is scared, it pretends to be dead. It lies on its back. It opens its mouth.

It even smells dead.
No animal wants to eat it!

BUSY BIRD

The Arctic tern flies from the South Pole to the North Pole. It rests there for a few months. Then it turns round and flies back.

It flies 800,000 kilometres
in its life!

RESCUE DOLPHINS

Dolphins can be kind and helpful. Some have saved people from sharks.

Some even lead boats to people in danger at sea.

WILD CAT

The margay wild cat likes to eat monkeys. It has a clever trick to catch them. It makes a noise like a baby monkey in danger.

Monkeys come to see what's wrong - then the cat eats them!

STRONG ANTS

Leafcutter ants work together to carry things. These ants can carry things 50 times heavier than they are.

They are very strong.

It is like you carrying a car!

INDEX

FOR TEACHERS

About SLIPSTREAM

Slipstream is a series of expertly levelled books designed for pupils who are struggling with reading. Its unique three-strand approach through fiction, graphic fiction and non-fiction gives pupils a rich reading experience that will accelerate their progress and close the reading gap.

At the heart of every Slipstream non-fiction book is exciting information. Easily accessible words and phrases ensure that pupils both decode and comprehend, and the topics really engage older struggling readers.

Whether you're using Slipstream Level 1 for Guided Reading or as an independent read, here are some suggestions:

1. Make each reading session successful. Talk about the text before the pupil starts reading. Introduce any unfamiliar vocabulary.

2. Encourage the pupil to talk about the book using a range of open questions. For example, what is their favourite animal and why?

3. Discuss the differences between reading non-fiction, fiction and graphic fiction. What do they prefer?

For guidance, SLIPSTREAM Level 1 – Super Animals has been approximately measured to:

National Curriculum Level: 2c
Reading Age: 7.0–7.6
Book Band: Turquoise
ATOS: 1.9*
Guided Reading Level: H
Lexile® Measure (confirmed): 440L

***Please check actual Accelerated Reader™ book level and quiz availability at www.arbookfind.co.uk**

Slipstream Level photocopiable WORKBOOK
ISBN: 978 1 4451 1609 9
available – download free sample worksheets from: www.franklinwatts.co.uk